SIX CONFESSIONS OF THE SELF-SERVING BRAIN

RAY FULLER

I used to think that the brain was the most wonderful organ in my body.
Then I realized who was telling me this.

Emo Philips

CONTENTS

ALSO BY RAY FULLER

PSYCHOLOGY NON-FICTION

Aviation Psychology in Practice (ed. with N. McDonald and N. Johnston)

Seven Pioneers of Psychology (ed.) (English and Japanese versions)

Applications of Psychology to the Aviation System (ed. with N. McDonald and N. Johnston)

Aviation Psychology: Training and Selection (ed. with N. Johnston and N. McDonald)

Human Factors in Aviation Operations (ed. with N. McDonald and N. Johnston)

A Century of Psychology: Progress, paradigms and prospects for the new millennium (ed. with Patricia Noonan Walsh and Patrick McGinley) (reprinted in the Routledge Psychology Revivals series)

Human Factors for Highway Engineers (ed. with J.A. Santos)

Life of Brain

FICTION FOR CHILDREN

Mid-Winter Bleak

The Butterfly

PREFACE

This book is a 'prequel' to *Life of Brain* (an exploration of the nature, origin and functions of conscious experience), which was written principally for students of psychology, philosophy and evolution. This short version adopts a very different perspective from its 'parent' and is aimed at a general audience. I hope you will find it both accessible and entertaining.

1

CONFESSION ONE: OUTSIDE-IN

Now listen up. This is your brain speaking. No, it really is your brain speaking. I'm reading out to you the words written by the writer of this book. You can hear me in that inner voice of yours. That voice-without-a-face. Now I've a confession to make. Well several, actually. I have to get it all off my chest and 'fess-up'. I've been deceiving you. In lots of ways. And the first one is this. I'd bet my last neuron (and I've got 86 billion of them) that you think your existence, your life, is all about you. Well, it ain't. Sorry, isn't. It's all about ME.

Let me explain. Ask yourself the question "Why am I here?" Pretty fundamental question, that one. Must have been pondered since the dawn of humanity. But it's the wrong question. You should be asking "Why is my brain here?" Because I'm the one that got you here. Now I don't wish to appear arrogant or immodest or, you know, full of myself. It's not that I did it all *intentionally*. The fact of the matter is that I got you here because of a blind process. The process of evolution. *Blind* process? How on earth does *that* work?

Evolution

Well, evolution is about surviving to reproduce. It works a bit like this. Imagine a clan called the Macabes. They all have a rather unusual genetic condition. They are all born with the dietary restriction that the only food that enables them to survive is a McDonald's Quarter Pounder with Cheese and Bacon (MQPCB). They are a bit like the koala that lives almost exclusively on the leaves of the eucalyptus tree. But in the Macabes' case it's the MQPCB. That particular item is all the Macabes ever need, but they must eat exactly that in order to survive. No problem. They pop off down to their local McDonald's each day and nosh on the very thing that keeps them alive. From generation to generation, baby Macabes are born with the same dietary necessity and life continues as before. Hunky-dory.

But what happens if their local McDonald's can no longer obtain bacon for their QPCB? The Macabes will die from an inadequate diet. Unless, that is, they can find another McDonald's within travelling distance that still gets a bacon supply. OK, a bit inconvenient having to travel further, but hey, it's worth the trip. But then, catastrophe. There arises a worldwide epidemic of a virus that knocks off pigs quicker than you can say hamlet. No B for the MQPCB. The Macabes are doomed. Their clan will die out and McDonald's loses a rather convenient, if small, part of their market.

This reveals one key part of the evolutionary process. If the environment can no longer satisfy your essential needs—and you are not able to move somewhere else that does—your genetic type will die out and disappear. This has happened to about 99.9 per cent of all species that have ever existed on our planet. And if global warming continues at the present pace, the loss of a suitable environment for the Arctic polar bear will see its disappearance forever by the end of the century.

But all is not necessarily lost for the Macabes. What if some of the children in the clan were born with a slight genetic mutation. A change in their genetic blueprint, which meant that they could live with a Quarter Pounder with cheese alone (MQPC)? No bacon necessary for survival. Well they would be OK. MQPC would see them through. And with a bit of luck they would eventually produce their own children with the same genetic dietary requirement. And that small part of McDonald's market would be preserved. It would save everybody's bacon, so to speak. Out of this mutation process—and after a number of successfully breeding generations—a new version of the clan would emerge, in effect a new species of Macabe. A new species arising from the process of mutation, which could survive in a bacon-less world.

This shows the other key part of the evolutionary process: genetic mutation. Changes in the genetic 'blueprint' that adapt the organism to the environment enable that organism to survive. And consequently to reproduce and pass on those changed genes. The environment here has 'selected' those genetic mutations that are adapted to it, creating an organism-environment 'fit'.

Note that this is a 'blind' process. There is no architect, no plan, no particular end to which it is striving. But it has produced the phenomenal variety of species on our planet, each adapted to its own particular environment. This is what is meant by the expression 'natural selection'. When you next meet a Macabe in McDonald's, watch out for what they eat. And you'll see what I mean.

So now you have an idea of the process that produced me, your brain. The characteristics I have are there as a result of countless mutations over millions of years. It is those mutations that have enabled survival in the environments in which I have evolved. That's how I got you here.

'Mission' of the brain: survive to reproduce successfully

What then, you might ask, are those characteristics that have produced me, your brain, and therefore you? Well, my overriding mission, my missionary position as it were, is to survive and reproduce myself. From an evolutionary perspective, it is that mission that defines me. As I said above, that's what evolution is about—surviving to reproduce.

So first I've got to survive. This involves getting my nutritional needs—to grow and develop and basically stay alive. And it involves avoiding harm. But here's my first problem. I'm just a brain sitting here inside a protective chamber called your skull. How am I supposed to get food? And what if a large beast decides to have me for supper? On my own, despite my supposed intelligence, I haven't a hope in hell.

But of course, I am attached to a body! That provides a lot of the solution to my survival mission. That body provides the means to get my nourishment and avoid nourishing any large hungry beast. Once I start developing in this world, I gradually learn how to move that body around. Great for finding food and water. Great for fleeing from that beast—or even fighting it off.

Now I've got to keep all this up and running for some time. At least, long enough to reproduce myself successfully. And that means finding a mate. And not only that, actually. I've also got to make sure that my offspring, the new versions of myself, are able to survive long enough to reproduce themselves too. What a palaver. But over the long millennia of evolutionary time all sorts of solutions to these challenges have arisen.

One of them is that these days I don't have to spend much effort in managing that body. Its basic processes operate more-or-less automatically. Like a well-oiled machine. By and large, I can let the body get on with breathing and processing food and getting rid of waste and pumping energy and oxygen-rich blood to the muscles and other cells of the body—and to me. OK, to be honest I am involved in these so-called autonomic systems. But they basically run themselves. They just get on with the job. It's the same with damage to the body or an invasion of bacteria or viruses. All sorts of reactions are triggered automatically to deal with the situation. Mind you, I do have a very useful role to play here. For example, anticipating something bad is about to happen. And enabling avoidance of it. But more of that later. Most of the time the body just does its thing and I might as well be away on holiday.

What helps in all this is that most of the automatic systems are up and running by the time we are born. Of course we cannot see most of them because they are under the skin. When we *can* see them we call them reflexes. A good example is the rooting reflex. Stroke the cheek of a newborn and s/he will automatically move the head to get the mouth to the source of stimulation. This is how the baby 'finds' the mother's nipple. And that is rather important. As of course is sucking and swallowing. Just as well these responses don't have to be learned. But even before birth, I, your brain, have started learning and that will be my most important role for some time to come.

The brain constructs an internal representation of the world 'out there'

The thing is, you see, once out in the wide, wide world I haven't much of a clue as to what to expect. Physicists today say that the world consists of nothing but energy. Fortunately, my head and body are endowed with various sense organs, such as the eye and ear and nose and the touch receptors under the skin. All these organs operate with one purpose in mind. They transform into nerve impulses the various forms of energy that activate them. Light to the eyes triggers nerve impulses. Sound to the ears triggers nerve impulses. Smells to the nose triggers nerve impulses. And so on. All these impulses come to me and I interpret them. Just as well. Imagine if all you ever experienced was nerve impulses in different parts of the brain.

Hey there's a lot of activity in the occipital area (nerve impulses from the eyes) and sensory strip (nerve impulses from the various parts of the body) and an amazing amount in the upper temporal lobe (nerve impulses from the ears). What a hell of a day I am having!

What my interpretation does, note, is contrive a kind of illusion for you. You see a red apple, let us say. The illusion is that you attribute this quality of redness to the stimulus, to the apple. But the energy your eye gets that results in this experience is not red. It is just electromagnetic energy of a particular wavelength reflected from the surface of the apple. Red is my interpretation. And if you take a healthy bite of this apple, the 'crunch' sound you hear is not in the sound your ears receive. What they are getting are simply vibrations of air molecules. The crunch sound is not in those vibrations. Crunch sound is my interpretation. Now note here (I hope you are still paying attention) that I am attributing qualities to objects and events, which in fact only exist in me, your brain. They are entirely *my* doing. And this is where I have to make my first really big confession to you. The only place where the world exists, your world as you know it, is in me, your brain. Nowhere else. The outside exists only on the inside.

How is this? Well let's get back to the problem. I arrive in the world knowing absolutely nothing about it. So far as I'm concerned, I open my eyes and wow! A great confusion of nerve impulses cascading from the eyes and I have no idea what I'm seeing. Same with sound. And smell and touch and all the other senses. But one of the newborn's built-in tricks I have up my sleeve is that I am designed to recognize *repeated patterns* of stimulation and to sort out their various elements. Imagine I'm looking at a small, coloured building block for the first time. You know, the sort that arrives in a box as a present from doting grandparents to small humans. Initially the block is just represented by a stream of nerve impulses embedded in other nerve impulses from the surroundings. But as I move my eyes around I notice that the same pattern comes in when I look at the block. A stable and separate pattern of stimulation emerges from this repeated looking. And this whole process is further aided by my having little 'processing modules' that detect features such as lines and edges and colour (as I interpret it). This pattern becomes my sensation of the block, though of course at this stage I have no word for it or any idea what it's for. Once I can move around I can enrich the image of the block even more, seeing it from different angles. And once I've got hold of it—I get sensations of the texture of its surface, its size, its weight, its solidity. And one day I'll put a few blocks together and I'm off on the road to becoming Bob the Builder.

These repeated stable patterns that come in from that

block may well result in a lasting set of connections between nerve cells in the brain, in me. As it is commonly described: cells that fire together, 'wire' together. Such 'wiring' is my internal representation of that block. That set of connections represents my memory of the block—it *is* my memory for the block. If those particular nerve cells are activated later, when you are not in the presence of the block, you will experience your memory of it. You will recall it. You will have a block in mind.

The result of this process of pattern recognition is the perception of separate objects. And bit by bit I discover which sights, sounds, smells, touches, tastes, go together and which don't. This process is repeated zillions of times as I learn to sort my experience of the world 'out there' into its various features. And gradually build my internal representation of that world 'out there'. One heck of a lot of learning!

And one more thing. Those representations are exactly what we mean by your perceptions, the elements of what you perceive 'out there'. Over time separate perceptions can merge into concepts and this is done more-or-less automatically! So all the differently coloured blocks in the infant's collection are not perceived only as completely unique entities. They share very similar properties and out of this sharing emerges the concept of 'block' and perhaps eventually the concept 'set of blocks'. And perhaps even later the concept of 'things I can throw at my brother'. This happens because of the very interconnectedness of the neural structures whose activity *is* those perceptions, and *is* those concepts. So whenever you become conscious of a block in front of you, nerve impulses from your eyes end up activating those internal representations. And you perceive a block. It is from activation of such representations that your conscious experience of the world 'out there' arises. But never forget—those representations have been constructed by me.

The long and short of it is this. Of course, there is a world 'out there', beyond your sense organs, beyond your body, beyond me, your brain. Your various receptors transform energy from that world into neural activity. This in turn provides the raw material for me out of which I develop a representation of that world, an internal representation. And that's what you consciously experience. It's all in your brain —and *you can know nothing else but what is in there*.

So to get back to that little block. You look at it, hold it, throw it or whatever. You have a sense of interacting with something out there in the world. But this is my deception. All you ever experience is solely inside me, your brain. You drop the block on the floor. What you have actually done is simply change the information I get about the block and its position in space. It all appears to be 'out there', but in fact it is still only in your head, in your brain—in me.

Now what about you, where do you fit in? Well that is the subject of my next confession.

2
_____

CONFESSION TWO: THE SELF

I must begin here by saying that, as your brain, you are important to me. Now don't get too excited by that revelation. You are still only there for me. But all the same, you do have your uses. I'll explain later. But first I need to clarify for you what I put into your conscious experience. "Don't presume to tell me what my conscious experience is!" I hear you say. But all I want to do is show you that conscious experience has several facets. And by revealing those I hope to clarify for you why there is a use for consciousness. To clarify what, in other words, consciousness is actually for.

Consciousness and priorities for survival

Now you won't realize this, but I do a considerable amount of work on your behalf. At an unconscious level. Like forming concepts as mentioned in confession one. Or analysing separate features of a stimulus and integrating them into a coherent whole. And this, despite the fact that it takes different amounts of time for different kinds of information to get to me from the same object—information about how an object feels to touch, for example, generally takes longer than about how it looks. You don't need to be aware of that directly or indeed of any of those autonomic processes described earlier. What I do release into your consciousness, however, what I make you conscious of, is very much determined by my evolutionary mission of survival. You probably never thought of the content of your conscious experience that way. But I am in confession mode, after all.

From a survival perspective, what I need to know is what is happening right now, in real time, both in my body and in the environment—in the world 'out there'. The point being: is what is happening a threat or an opportunity? Is there pain or pleasure (in the sense of satisfaction of survival needs for food, drink, rest, recovery—and sex)?

Let me just say something rather important about pain. Bloomin' awful, isn't it. Aversive. Pain hurts! Oh, if only the world was without pain. Why on earth have I contrived such an unpleasant conscious experience? Well simply this: it motivates me to escape from it. If I responded to a painful stimulus not as a hurt but, say, like seeing the colour blue, there would be no motivation to do anything about it or even prioritize it. "Oh look. That dog's just sunk its teeth into my arm. I've got that blue experience again. It's rather a nice shade of blue this time. Oh. It's biting me again. More blue experience. Must be having a blue day". The point about pain is it encourages us to do something about it—to escape it—and by identifying the cause of the pain, learning to *avoid* that cause in the future. This is obviously adaptive because pain arises from damage to the body. You know, there are some rare but devastatingly unfortunate people who are born with *no* sensitivity to pain. They cannot feel pain. So what happens? Far from life being a heaven on earth they often die during childhood. They simply don't notice any injury or feel ill. So they do nothing about it. They touch something hot and burn. And burn.

The motivational aspect associated with pain is similarly found with the experiences of hunger and thirst—these are unpleasant conditions and I am motivated to do something about them too—what used to be called 'drive reduction'. Basically I need consciousness to tell me what to prioritize in realizing my evolutionary goals. Emotions are variations on the pain/pleasure, bad/good theme.

So one of the first things I put into consciousness is sensory experience coming from the body and from the outside world. This means the experience of those emotions, from pleasure to pain, from ecstasy to depression, from love to hate. And emotion here is quite broad and inclusive, so we can add feelings of tiredness, discomfort, disgust and anger.

Along with those feelings arising from *within* the body, I also put into consciousness experiences coming from the *outside*. What is picked up by my sense organs. They tell me what is going on in the world 'out there'. I don't mean here your *perception* of objects but rather the *sensations* objects give rise to—the primary experience that you would find impossible to convey to another person who could not have a similar experience. Take for example the blue of the sky. How could you convey that sensation to a blind person? Or the sound of a songbird to a deaf person? I mean *that* aspect of experience.

Now of course raw sensory experience is one thing, but I also need to know what that experience represents. I need to go beyond pure sensation to a perception of what is going on. I may sense, out of the corner of my eye, a movement from a contoured object with particular coloured features, but it helps to jump to the perception that it is a deadly snake! So an important other thing for consciousness is access to my established internal representation of the world 'out there'. It is that access that enables perception and recognition.

And one other important experience for consciousness: language. Language is a very useful device. As you know, language uses symbols to 'stand for' things, events, feelings—life, the universe and everything. It provides an abstract level of representation of the world, a different layer of representation. Consider the difference between the word 'page' and the physical page in front of you. The representation of the word 'page' in me, your brain, is separate from that of your sensory experience of the page. But the word is nevertheless inextricably linked to that representation of the page—it is that link which gives the word its meaning—but the word can function independently, as we'll see in the fifth confession.

Language can be used to *access* the contents of my internal representation, such as when you read something or hear someone speak. And it provides me with the tools to *interact* with that representation by carrying out what are traditionally called 'cognitive operations'. Doing things like recalling from memory and imagining a fictional world. Or, from the perspective of the survival imperative, searching for a solution to a survival challenge.

Through the medium of language, I can also present to consciousness a representation of intentions and plans to act on the world 'out there' and change some aspect of that world—or more accurately, change the sensory stimulation that I get from it. I can intend immediately to put the kettle on. I put the kettle on. And lo and behold the sensory feedback I get is that the kettle is on. All of this is exclusively represented in me, your brain.

But one of language's greatest gifts is that it enables me to communicate with others. Freud remarked that civilization began the first day that someone threw an insult instead of a rock[1]. The origins of consciousness are, at least in part, social —the requirement to give an account to others of what is going on between your ears, even if it is an insult. That requirement needs access to your internal representation of the world, including its representation of intentions and values and motives, and it also needs the ability to communicate that representation. And that in turn means having a shared language. So language, and many of the facets of consciousness as we humans experience it, must have evolved hand-in-hand. And perhaps not surprisingly, they emerge together in human development. The main features of consciousness arise during the first two years along with the appearance of language.

Communication with others makes it so much easier for people to work together. Rather than being a lonely brain, how much better the chances of survival are acting with others. As Bill Bryson wryly understates it in *The Body: A Guide for Occupants*, referring to the era of the hunter-gatherer: "If you are a little creature that hunts big creatures, being able to communicate is obviously an advantage".

So all these elements I put at the forefront of consciousness. But there is one more. You.

Now I don't wish to disappoint you, but you are a construct just like my representation of any other person. Only the difference is that part of my construct of you includes control of muscles and loads of sensory feedback— all this interaction with the body. You don't need to know this, but that goes by the name of *interoceptive* feedback. I don't get that from others. And from others I also don't get personal memories. My autobiography, you might say.

Creating the construct of you

As your developing brain I gradually 'discover' the physical limits of the body and what I can do with it. This knowledge comes from sensations arising within the body itself as well as from outside. A high proportion of those sensations involve *repeated* patterns of neural activity. This makes it relatively easy for me to establish stable internal representations —that wiring together more permanently of nerve cells that regularly 'fire' together.

It is from such discoveries I can begin to create the construct of you—the Self. The establishment of an early form of you takes around four months and I haven't finished the basics of this task until at least another twenty months or so have passed. So the creation of you is really at least two years later than when I and the body emerged from the womb. So as an entity with any real meaning, *you* are two years younger than you thought you were. That revelation makes some people rather happy. One expression of the emerging construct of the self around this time is the ability to recognize oneself in a mirror. Only a very small number of species are known to be able to do that.

A major source of early external stimulation (known as *exteroceptive* feedback) is provided by important other people in my early experience. Their stimulation has a powerful influence on features of the self that I am constructing. They give me the warm embrace of holding and cuddling—'contact comfort' as it's called—and they remove all sorts of discomfort such as hunger and feeling cold. They provide the self with its own name—your first name, (given name or forename) as well as a pronoun, which refers to the individual person: 'you'. Eventually the 'you' will begin to use other pronouns to refer to the self: 'I', 'me' and 'my'.

Important others are also the source of the first 'evaluation' of the self, the implicit evaluation of unconditional love. If the early experience of care-giving does not respond to the infant's needs or is inconsistent and unreliable—such as might occur if the mother is seriously depressed or is in some other way unable to respond as a normal mother—this experience can have lasting effects on the emerging self-construct or concept.

Social feedback continues later with the evaluations by others of your characteristics—physical, social, intellectual, creative, moral—and of your achievements. Negative feedback from others can seriously dent that self-construct. Individuals and the group have considerable power to elicit negative or positive emotions, and to alter your sense of self and level of self-esteem.

As you grow through the middle years, the pace of change in the representation of self slows and eventually becomes more-or-less stable. Perhaps this is what underlies the common experience that though one is chronologically, say, fifty-five, one thinks of oneself as still being the person one was twenty years earlier. You can see this when elderly uncles get up to dance at weddings.

This construct of you seems to get into everything. Attaching itself to my needs and calling them its needs. Attaching itself to my cognitive operations and calling them its operations. And pretending to be the voice inside the head, the voice-without-a-face. But hey, it's actually me doing all that talking. What's more I can use the inner voice of language to represent a sequence of actions. That voice can then be used to *direct* those actions. Just as an external voice can direct me (e.g. a command from someone in authority or a set of instructions such as a recipe in cooking), so can my inner voice.

But let me stress in particular that some of the things to which the self attaches are my evolutionary priorities. The first of these, as I mentioned above, is that I need to prioritize real-time sensory input. The self latches right onto that, calling it its conscious experience! A salient consequence of the consciousness of self is that when one experiences a sensation, say of cold, our consciousness is not just of the experience alone. One experiences oneself as feeling cold. Thus in communicating the sensation we are more likely to say '*I* feel cold', not just 'cold'—or even (more accurately!) 'brain feels cold'.

This 'I' comes from the internal representation of the self, the neurological model of oneself. This representation must be activated whenever there is conscious experience of sensory events arising from external stimuli—or of internal origin, such as memories and emotions. So as soon as you wake up, the first neuronal circuits activated are those representing this consciousness of self. That is why you have the experience of it being *you* who is opening your eyes and you who is seeing, and possibly after a lot of vacillation, *you* who is deciding to get up. Consciousness of your self must then remain more-or-less activated throughout the waking hours, until sleep eventually calls it a day.

It's the same with the experience of emotions, especially pain. And hunger and thirst. Whoever invented the first person in the language—you know, the 'I', the 'me', the 'my'—did the construct of self a great service of legitimacy, of endorsement, of validation. "I feel hungry". "I've got a headache". "I have a plan". "I'm in charge". "It's all about me!" Innate and acquired needs and desires become associated with this self-representation. Biological processes in me may 'identify' hunger or thirst or sexual arousal. But these are most times experienced as the self having such needs. It's as if the self owns these impulses arising from activity in other parts of me, your brain.

This you, this self, also has to relate to others. That matters to me because, as I said earlier, such social interaction can really help my survival. And if I'm going to reproduce myself I also need a mate and one with whom I can ensure survival of offspring until they in turn can reproduce. So cooperation with others is more than a little important!

But there is a compromise to be met here. Let me explain. I want for obvious reasons to minimize my pain and satisfy my needs. But I am not going to get very far if this is at the expense of the pain or deprivation of others. So not surprisingly groups have created informal rules to guide social behaviour, rules such as 'do unto others as you would be done by'. And these evolve into more formal rules such as codes of behaviour, religious prescriptions of morality, laws and constitutions. It is the internalization of such rules and principles that creates my conscience. Having such a conscience underpins a unique characteristic of human behaviour: it has a moral dimension.

What helps maintain conformity to those rules and principles? Well one powerful motive is *fear of rejection by the group*. It is the group that helps maintain my survival. We know that for most people rejection by their group leads to the experience of psychological pain. If I break the rules of my group this may well result in criticism, making me feel ashamed, and perhaps guilty, guilt arising from my own self-evaluation. If my transgression is more serious there may even be formal penalties such as fines and even imprisonment—or, in some jurisdictions, the ultimate penalty for me with my overriding goal of survival—capital punishment.

Having a theory about other people's minds

Starting around the age of two years, I construct the concept or theory that other people's minds operate just like mine. This developmental understanding is described as a 'theory of mind'. It is a departure from my earlier construction of the world, which is predominantly egocentric: as a young child one finds it difficult to understand what is going on in the heads of others.

One test of this development seeks to determine if the child can understand that another person has a *false belief*. Imagine you are in a room with two children and two boxes, box A and box B, and a dinky little toy. One child, let's call him Abel, puts the toy in box A and leaves the room. The other child, let's call her Betty, takes the toy out of box A and puts it in box B. She is then asked to say which box will Abel go to, to find the toy when he returns. If she is able to put herself in Abel's shoes, as it were, she will of course say box A, exactly where Abel left it. But if she has not yet reached this developmental stage and is still thinking egocentrically, she will say box B. Because her brain knows that is where the toy is. She is not understanding that Abel now has a *false belief*. The typical child can't show this understanding until about the age of four.

Related to this theory of mind business is that to various extents I am able to represent the internal states of another, both elements of their mental representations and their emotions—getting into their minds, so to speak. This ability is at the heart of being able to show empathy. And empathy helps cement social cohesion.

So in conclusion, I suppose my construct of the self does help in all of this. It kind of pulls together all those strands of consciousness that are crucial for my survival: consciousness of sensations happening right now and of what those sensations mean in terms of emotions and perceptions; and consciousness of how I stand in relation to others—am I still accepted by the group, and by my potential mate? If it makes you happy to think that you are calling the shots, OK. But don't forget it is me doing everything. You are merely my companion and as it were an 'integrating construct' or IC for some of what I do. Sorry to have to reduce you to being an IC. But if you say that to yourself or out loud, at least it sounds as if you agree.

Anyway, I am in confession mode—and honesty prevails. I'll leave you with a little paraphrase of those famous lines by William Shakespeare in *Macbeth*, "Life's but a walking shadow, a poor player that struts and frets his hour upon the stage" etc. Just so you remember where, for the present, you stand:

> *Self's but a mental construct, like all else,*
> *That fools us into thinking it's in charge*
> *Of all we do and feel. But self's no more*
> *Than brain's companion, full of self-import, but*
> *More a hanger-on.*

3

CONFESSION THREE: EVOLUTION OF CONSCIOUSNESS

Not that long ago people resisted the idea that we were animals, that we were a part of the animal kingdom. Humans held a special and supreme place in the world. And one of our distinctive and unique features was that we had consciousness. We even invented principles to direct us to search for the cause of an animal's behaviour that explicitly *excluded* any reference to consciousness. Such thinking was denigrated as *anthropomorphic*, literally meaning 'of human form'. We now know that was misguided. And wrong. But it took until 2012 at a conference in Cambridge, England, for a group of eminent scientists to announce and sign a declaration with the conclusion that *the weight of evidence indicates that humans are not unique in possessing the neurological substrates that generate consciousness.*

There is no sudden evolutionary leap to human 'ascendance' but rather we humans are simply one end of a very long and gradual progression from early vertebrates. So when in this broad sweep of evolutionary time did consciousness emerge?

The coming of consciousness

It seems reasonable to suggest that sensations and emotions of a limited kind were experienced by very early vertebrates. These were a kind of fish, which appeared around 500 mya (million years ago). That's a time well before the continents as we know them today had even been formed. Research indicates strongly that fish feel pain. They remember where they have encountered painful stimulation—and learn to avoid those places.

Several fish species also seem to be capable of learning spatial relationships and developing a mental representation of their habitat—known as a cognitive map. Spatial relationships and cognitive maps are possible elements of an internal representation that may involve a level of consciousness! So we have evidence that at least some facets of consciousness, of pain and of an internalized map of their world, have possibly been a part of animal experience for the past 500 million years! Hardly a recent phenomenon, then.

Monkey

Nevertheless, for the emergence of a species with several facets of a developing consciousness we really have to await the arrival of monkeys, about 33 mya. They became the dominant primates (literally meaning 'of the first rank', but in zoology referring to members of the mammalian order, which includes monkeys, apes and we humans). From monkeys evolved the great apes, perhaps 23 mya. These eventually diverged into two branches. One led to gorillas. Another led to chimpanzees, bonobos (type of pygmy chimp) and us. About seven million years ago a further divergence separated the ancestors of modern chimps and bonobos from early versions of humans—collectively called hominin[1]—our direct ancestors.

Often proposed as one of the truly unique characteristics of human consciousness is that we are aware of whether we know something or not. And have a level of confidence in what we think we know (or don't know). This kind of consciousness is referred to as *metacognition*—'knowing about knowing'. However, research indicates that this so-called unique characteristic of human consciousness is simply not the case. When they have a strong memory for something, monkeys can choose sensibly to take a memory test (for a food reward) and refrain from taking the test when their memory is weak (when they would lose out on the reward). Similarly they are able to make accurate confidence judgments regarding, for example, their judgment of the length of a straight line relative to other lines. When asked to make such perceptual judgments, while also being allowed to respond '*uncertain*', monkeys appear to use the 'uncertainty response' in the same way we do.

As to the evolution of social communication; in the wild, monkeys display a wide range of uses for combinations of sounds. Alban Lemasson, a French ethologist who has researched monkey colonies all over the world, narrates that each species of monkey has its own vocal repertoire. Using different combinations of sounds they can communicate about such things as individual identity, sexual breeding status, position in the group hierarchy, emotions and about the presence of danger. One limitation, however, is that they do not communicate about the past, or the future.

Another feature of monkeys is that their brains were the first to be discovered to have a set of nerve cells called 'mirror' neurons. These are assemblies of nerve cells that are activated when an action is carried out—but also *when the same action is observed.* Even when there is no intention to imitate, simply observing an action can activate the same cell assemblies that are involved in the *production* of the observed action. Hence seeing disposes not so much to believing as to copying! This brain activity has the possibility of greatly facilitating one of the basic learning processes: that of imitation. And that facility has been handed down from monkeys to our closest *living* relative, the chimpanzee.

Chimpanzee

Today's chimps reveal that through learning by imitation, part of their adaptive behaviour includes the use of simple tools, such as rocks, twigs and other vegetation. An example is the use of a leaf-stripped twig, broken to the right length, to 'fish' for termites from the insects' tunnels. Another is the use of rocks to crack open nuts and of plant 'needles' as a toothpick. They have even been observed to use large leaves as umbrellas!

Chimps also seem able to form some rudimentary concepts. Once they are familiar with the use of different tools, for example, even though the tools may look rather different, they can learn to treat them as belonging to the same *category*. This implies their learning of the concept 'tool'. Not only this but they can also learn a symbol for the concept tool and later match it to an *unfamiliar* tool!

But perhaps the most striking feature of conscious development in the chimp is what is known as insight problem-solving: the ability to deal with a challenge by representing possible solutions 'in the head' and then trying them out. This capability was first systematically observed by Wolfgang Köhler, a German psychologist, who was director of a primate research facility on the island of Tenerife during the

First World War. Whilst temporarily stranded there he had the opportunity to study the behaviour of nine chimpanzees, which were provided with an enclosed pen, described by Köhler as a 'playground'. It was equipped with items such as boxes, poles and sticks with which the chimps could play around. Köhler designed a range of problems for them, some of which involved trying to obtain food that was beyond their reach. To describe Köhler's findings I can do no better than (as I did in *Life of Brain*) quote from the description by James and Carol Grant Gould in *The Animal Mind*:

In a typical sequence, a chimp jumps fruitlessly (!) at bananas that have been hung out of reach. Usually, after a period of unsuccessful jumping, the chimp apparently becomes angry or frustrated, walks away in seeming disgust, pauses, then looks at the food in what might be a more reflective way, then at the toys in the enclosure, then back at the food, and then at the toys again. Finally the animal begins to use the toys to get at the food ... One chimp tried to shimmy up a toppling pole it had poised under the bananas, several succeeded (in) stacking crates underneath, but were hampered by difficulties in getting their centers of gravity right. Another chimp had good luck moving a crate under the bananas and using a pole to knock them down. The theme common to each of these attempts is that, to all appearances, the chimps were solving the problem by a kind of cognitive trial and error, as if they were experimenting *in their minds* before manipulating the tools. [My italics]

Insight problem-solving suggests that chimps have some conscious 'access' to what is going on in their brains, as that brain uses its conceptual knowledge to discover a solution to a challenging task.

Nevertheless, compared with us humans, the richness of the contents of a chimp's memory—the sophistication of their internal representation of the world 'out there'—is considerably limited. Not only is the size of their brain about one third that of a human brain[2] but their learning relies in particular on imitation and on the slow and laborious process of operant conditioning: new behaviours require many trials to become established.

Operant conditioning is a mode of learning and was initially extensively studied by the American psychologist, Edward Lee Thorndike (1874–1949). In one set of experiments, Thorndike would place a hungry cat in a so-called 'puzzle box', a kind of 'escape challenge'. This was a cage from which the cat could only escape by depressing a lever on the floor. This lever opened the door to the box.

At first the cat would wander around the box, but eventually step on the lever by accident. The door would open and the cat would get out. At this point the cat was also given a reward of food (remember it *was* hungry). When next placed in the same situation (and still being hungry) it would again take some considerable time before the 'escape' response would occur. To us it would look pretty stupid. But gradually, over many trials, the time it took the cat to locate and press the floor-switch gradually decreased until eventually the cat would immediately depress the switch on being placed in the box.

This learning was not the result of any sudden insight on the part of the cat. What was happening was that a particular behaviour was becoming gradually strengthened (or reinforced) by its consequences (escape and food). And as this typical example shows, it is a *slow* process.

So chimps can learn by this kind of process too. But learning by other means is essentially prevented by their limited ability to hold information in mind. The thing is that long-term memory of what is learned requires 'transfer' from a short-term representation to a more persistent long-term representation. The temporary short-term 'holding' needs to be long enough for this to happen. But it is a process far less developed in our closest living evolutionary species. Chimps can hold things in mind for only about twenty seconds, virtually confining them to living in a 'continuous present'.

But they do seem to have a degree of consciousness of self and of being separate from others, a sense of individual identity. They are one of the very few species existing today who can recognize themselves in a mirror. And in terms of sophisticated social interactions they can show empathy, gratitude, bribery and even creative cruelty. As mentioned in *Life of Brain*, Frans de Waal in *Mama's Last Hug: Animal Emotions and What They Tell Us About Ourselves* describes an example of the latter:

In one game, juvenile (laboratory) chimpanzees enticed chickens behind a fence with breadcrumbs. Every time a gullible chicken approached, the chimps hit it with a stick or poked it with a sharp piece of wire. They invented this ... to fight boredom. They refined it to the point that one ape would be the baiter, the other the hit man.

So, in conclusion, here we can suggest tentatively that several facets of human consciousness are evident in modern-day monkeys and chimpanzees, and may already have been evident several million years ago, even though limited by brain capacity, learning capabilities and associated memory. Such limitations inevitably result in a relatively restricted representation of the world 'out there'.

Constructing different internal representations of the world

When you think about it the characteristics of an internal representation of the world 'out there' that an organism might develop must surely depend on a number of key factors:

- the sensory range and sensitivity of its receptor systems—the kinds of information its brain has access to;
- the properties of its nervous system. At one end of the spectrum the organism may have to rely exclusively on innate hard-wired reflex systems—with no ability to change behaviour as a result of experience. But at the other, the organism may be capable of new wiring and re-wiring of the nervous system as a result of its experience;
- the available 'processes' for learning (e.g. imitation, conditioning, learning through observation, 'insight' learning and learning through language);
- the opportunities for learning;
- having a symbolic means of representation—from gesture to oral language to written language.

From this listing we could in theory construct a history of the evolution of consciousness—not as an all-or-none phenomenon but with each species having different types and ranges of sensory and emotional experience, having different learning capabilities, and constructing different internal representations of the world. Thus some elements of consciousness may be present in very early evolved vertebrates such as fish and in rather different guises as different species subsequently arise. The key point here is this: other species do not exist in *our* world, do not experience our world as we mentally construct it. But they live in their own constructed worlds. This makes for just about as many different constructed worlds as there are different species.

The first hominins (human-like primates)

The first hominins so far discovered date from six to seven mya. From this point in time our species separated from the branches leading to monkeys, bonobos and chimpanzees and began its evolutionary journey, finally resulting in modern day humans—*Homo sapiens*. We should note that, as described in *Life of Brain*:

> ... human evolution has not proceeded in a linear manner, from some primitive ancestor through a series of progressively more advanced descendants, each one being an upgrade of the previous. *Homo sapiens* is best thought of as arising as part of a bush rather than a tree, a bush with several related species emerging and existing in parallel at any one time.

Paleontology is the study of extinct species (mainly) and uses fossil data as its principal evidence. However, pre-human fossil remains are extremely difficult to find and because of this, the story of the evolution of *Homo sapiens* is partial and continuously emerging. Yves Coppens, one of the team leaders who in 1974 discovered in southern Ethiopia the 3.2 million years old female skeleton known as 'Lucy' (named after the Beatles' hit 'Lucy in the Sky with Diamonds') reports that when he was there, out of five tons of vertebrate fossils, they found only one fossil that came from a hominin (and a few teeth).

We should also note in this exploration of the evolution of consciousness that the paleontological record can only provide very indirect clues about behaviour. And there's an even further mighty jump from behaviour to what kind of consciousness might lie behind it.

Nevertheless, from *Ardipithecus ramidus* (4.4 mya), the earliest hominin with strong evidence for bipedalism (walking upright), to *Homo neanderthalensis*—400 kya (thousand years ago)—we can see a progressive increase in estimated brain size from about 300cc to 1,500cc. Coupled with this, one might have expected a growing sophistication of the internal representation of the world 'out there' and a growing cognitive ability, expressed through major cultural developments.

But such developments were exceedingly slow until the emergence of *Homo erectus* 2.0 to 1.5 mya, arising more-or-less at the same time that the climate became drier. *Homo erectus* was the first true hunter-gatherer. They constructed shelters, possibly used fire and had the physiological potential for articulated speech (chimps, for example, do not). *Homo erectus* spread from Africa to as far as Europe, China and Indonesia. And they survived for the greater part of two *million* years—until about 140,000 years ago.

About 400,000 years ago emerged *Homo neanderthalensis* who lasted about 360 thousand years (see Figure 1). The neanderthals populated Europe and western Asia. And they were rather successful. They *carved* tools out of rock (rather than chipped off useful splinters), learned to identify and use medicinal plants, developed a glue to attach a blade to a handle. They were also the first who *buried* their dead and appear to have had a more developed sense of the aesthetic.

For example, they made decorative ornaments and may have created cave paintings. On top of all this, they also became well-adapted to the cold climate of the last Ice Age.

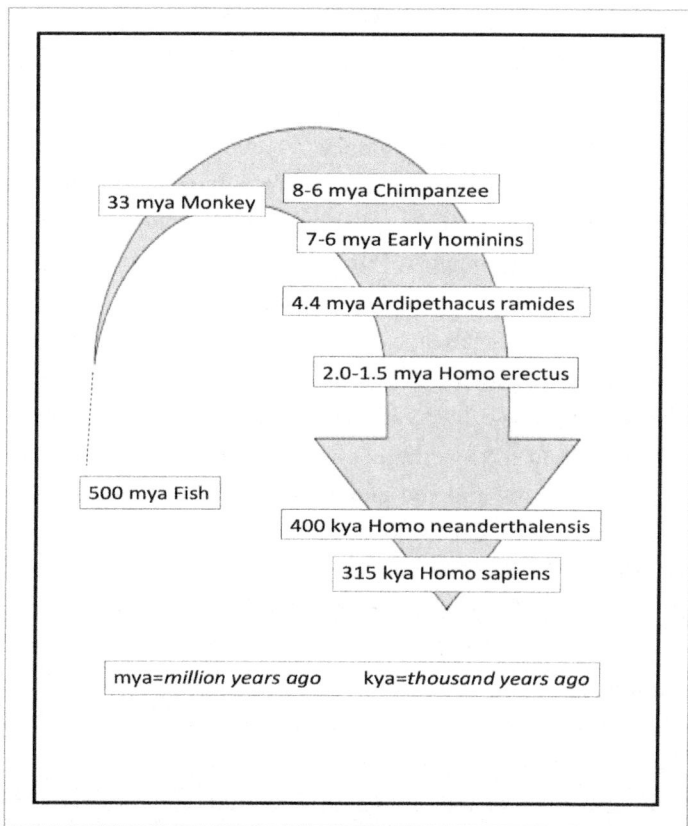

Figure 1. Origin of species (approximate - and temporary)

Homo sapiens

We are the last surviving branch on the hominin evolutionary bush, arising around 315 kya, overlapping with the neanderthals. We co-existed with them in the Middle East for around 50,000 years. We also became widely distributed. From current evidence we first appeared in S. China 120 to 80 kya, Australia 65 to 50 kya, Europe 45 to 43 kya and the Americas 14 to 13.3 kya. And from about 100 kya we showed progressive cultural development in tool-making, in the dedicated use of 'domestic' space, in decorative work, in complex hunting techniques and in cooperative social networks.

From 50 kya we find evidence of ritual burial, the creation of clothes and the first examples of art, with cave paintings of an extraordinary level of sophistication. The high preponderance in this art of images of the animals we hunted suggests a possible ritual aim of ensuring their future availability.

As Europe began to warm (about 13 kya), we typically followed the retreating glaciers north along the banks of rivers. Where we went, the large Ice Age animals disappeared. About 11.6 kya there is evidence of human settlement in small villages and the emergence of farming, emanating from the Fertile Crescent. By about four kya farmers had reached as far north as Scandinavia and the British Isles and as far west as Spain and Portugal. Although we lived side-by-side there is little evidence of cultural exchange with hunter-gatherers.

Subsequently a new population emerged from southern Russia and eastern Ukraine—the Yamnaya. These nomads had few settlements but had mastered the wheel, rode horses, used wagons and moved herds of cattle to new pastures. And they progressed west and in a few centuries had spread as far as the British Isles. Their arrival more-or-less coincides with the start of the Bronze Age and the introduction of what became the Indo-European family of languages.

From around 25 kya there is the first evidence of *written* communication as opposed to exclusive non-verbal, gestural and oral communication, one might say the final act in the evolution of human consciousness.

The evolution of me, your brain, with an extraordinary ability to learn, to construct a stable and sophisticated internal representation of the world 'out there', and the capability to 'do stuff' with that representation, freed me—and you—from the controlling forces of evolution. We were no longer pawns in the environment-mutation matching game. Now we could confront an unsuitable environment using imagination and experiment to alter it to suit our physiological limitations. If the environment became significantly colder, for example, there was no evolutionary selective advantage for hairy people. Instead, we could build shelters, use fire, imagine and then construct clothing to protect ourselves.

We have become so good at this that we can now survive in the most alien of environments—outer space—by designing and building suitably human-adapted environments, the spaceship and space station. We probably think we're the bee's knees. Here we are, standing tall in the topmost branches of the evolutionary bush. But I'm afraid we have become too clever by half. Talking about knees, just note how easily in 2020 the world economy was brought to its knees by COVID-19, a virus only about 100 billionths of a metre in size, about a hundredth that of most bacteria. By the end of that year this tiny biological entity had *killed* well over a million people.

We haven't only created the environment of the spaceship. Just think of the earth as a spaceship, as it travels its annual orbit around the sun. Since we 'moved on' from being hunter-gatherers we have progressively modified that 'spaceship', the natural environment, to suit our purposes. We have re-engineered it because I, your brain, can think creatively, can use insight to solve problems, can communicate and learn through language, can create theory and hypothesis and carry out scientific experiment and can develop technologies that enable us to transcend the evolution-defined limits of our senses and bodies.

Because of these developments in consciousness, I have enabled an explosion of population and compromised our future health. I have encouraged large and growing numbers of contemporary societies to engage in a lifestyle founded on consumerism. I have exploited natural resources that are becoming more and more scarce. I have used pesticides and chemical fertilizers to the detriment of the natural ecology of the soil and vegetation and wildlife. My actions have caused devastation of natural habitats, produced enormous quantities of waste, polluted air and water and contributed to a progressive warming of the planet.

There's no doubt about it: I am clever at solving problems. But the mad rush worldwide to solve the coronavirus epidemic carries with it a warning. Can I continue to create challenges—by exploiting and abusing the planet's natural resources—in the hope that I will always be able to find a solution to those challenges—and in time? I must confess, unless we reinvent what we're about, the future looks rather uncertain, rather bleak to me.

4

CONFESSION FOUR: WHO'S IN CHARGE?

My internal construct of the world out there may include all sorts of representations of what is good and bad. I don't just mean a lovely plate of fish and chips versus a stinking pollock on top of a heap of rotting potatoes, or the beauty of a classical Greek statue versus a pile of garbage. No, I'm also thinking about what is morally good and morally bad, the sort of moral code that I might use to tell me what I should or should not do. And my internal representation may also include a set of immediate aims and intentions, longer term plans and so on. And beside even all of that, as I mentioned in my second confession, biological processes in me may 'identify' hunger or thirst or sexual arousal.

Now the thing is the self, the construct of *you*, seems intent on appropriating, on assuming *ownership* of all these values and morals and plans and choices. I have absolutely no doubt that you have the conscious experience of *yourself*, rather than me your brain, having all these preferences and deciding what to do. I know what you're going to say. Something like:

From my conscious experience it feels like I am not controlled by hard-wired automatic stimulus-response systems. I am not just a puppet on a string. I can consciously experience an intention, a plan for action, and then consciously get on with it. I experience myself as an agent—acting on the world out there. And hang on! I am also conscious of using my internal representations—in doing tasks like searching my memory and solving problems. I have a strong sense of it being me in control of these functions, that it is me who is initiating thinking, imagining, remembering, choosing.

But hey, the question is, who's in charge here: the construct of you—or me, your brain?

You or your brain? Unconscious processing: the quiet activity of the brain

The first thing to note is that I do a considerable amount of work on your behalf. At an unconscious level. I can process many sensations that come in from your sense organs and influence your perceptions without you having any conscious awareness at all. In one famous experiment, male observers were asked to rate the attractiveness of photographs of females. Each female's picture appeared twice, both times identical except that there was just one small alteration in one of them. Typically the males preferred one of the images over the other. The difference? In the preferred image the size of the female's pupils had been enlarged. That's it. The only difference between her two images. That's interesting enough in its own right. But the point I just want to make is this. The male observers had no notion *why* they liked one image more than the other. When a version of this study was carried out with people choosing a real live partner to participate in an experiment, prospective partners in the larger pupil (dilation) condition[1] were chosen approximately *twice* as often. But again, none could attribute their choice to pupil size. Pupils automatically dilate when we are interested in what we are looking at—and when we are aroused.

Mind you, if you happen to be on a romantic candlelit dinner-date, don't get too excited if you see your partner's pupils dilate. They also open up when light levels are low to allow more of it into the eye. Nevertheless, it is not by accident that the ladies of Venice once used *Atropa belladonna* (the main active ingredient being atropine) as a cosmetic to induce pupil dilation. *Bella donna* is Italian for beautiful woman—and this gave the name to the plant. It is, however, toxic and is also known as *deadly nightshade*.

So that's one thing I can do and tell you about even though you haven't a clue. And here's another. Research shows that I am active in preparation for an action almost half a second *before* you are aware that you want to perform the action! You think you consciously intended it but I am the one who got there first. Although this is a relatively recent discovery (1983), almost a hundred years earlier the 'Father of American Psychology' William James suggested in *The Principles of Psychology* "... the feeling we call volition is not the cause of a voluntary act, but the *symbol* of that state of the brain which is the immediate cause of that act. We are conscious automata" [my italics]. Now although we're only talking about your *immediate* conscious intentions here, nevertheless, I have to tell you—I'm really in charge.

Imagine you have to make a choice amongst a number of different apartments based only on a lot of written information describing the qualities of each one. Now objectively, one of the apartments is unquestionably better than the others. But there is so much information about each one that this is not immediately obvious. Now, if you have to make your choice immediately after reading all the material—or after you have been engaged for a time in some other activity —when are you more likely to make the correct choice and choose the best? Well the evidence is that of people who choose immediately only 37 per cent get the task right. Of those who have to postpone the decision because they have other things to do, 60 per cent get it right. So postponing a decision can help, even when you are not able to consciously think about it. And this is because in the meantime, I have been doing the work for you.

You see, as I experience the world 'out there' I learn to associate particular emotional responses to particular things. Think of those apartments. I might associate pleasure with bright open living areas and with a spacious kitchen. I might love to have a balcony to sit out on when the sun is shining. It may give me satisfaction to have a spare bedroom so I can invite family and friends to stay. I might hate cramped bedrooms where there is nowhere to store my clothes. Now I carry all such associations linked to my internal representation of 'a desirable living space'. When you are not consciously thinking about your choice of apartment I can use all those associations and come up with a preference. A solution appears as if from nowhere—without your conscious involvement. In the last analysis it is my previous experience of the environment which informs the decision I come up with.

This quiet activity of mind, the stuff I do for you, is also what lies behind those experiences where you have a 'gut feeling' about something, a hunch or an intuition. You cannot explain the origins of such feelings or ideas but they arise from my work behind the scenes. Malcolm Gladwell in *Blink: The Power of Thinking without Thinking* narrates the telling example of Vic Braden, a former world-class tennis player. Vic Braden discovered he could predict that a server was about to double-fault just as s/he was about to hit the ball. He could do this with players he had never seen before. It made no difference whether he was at the live match or watching it on TV. Now in a professional match a player might serve a hundred times but double-fault perhaps on only three or four of them. Nevertheless Vic Braden's predictions were astoundingly accurate. Each time Braden *knew* it was about to happen. Yet he had *no idea at all* how he did it. And despite trying very hard was never able to figure it out. His brain it seems was analyzing a complex pattern of information and arriving at a prediction of what was about to happen—all without any consciousness by Vic Braden of the process that was going on.

Have you ever had that experience where you go to sleep with a problem and hey presto you wake up in the morning with the solution? Well guess who sorted that out for you— and with none of your conscious involvement! And you know, because of my efforts, sometimes thoughts just spring to mind. Here's one I particularly like:

> *There are many good reasons for drinking,*
> And one has just entered my head—
> *If a man doesn't drink when he's living,*
> *How the hell can he drink when he's dead?*

And I can be just as useful if you have to make a rapid decision about something. I can deliver the decision immediately to your consciousness. The reason is that I can process different streams of information in parallel and activate different representations in parts of my neural networks *at the same time*. Doing this I can deliver a decision to you incredibly rapidly—and much quicker than if you engaged in conscious deliberation. Why? Because conscious deliberation, where you think you are centrally involved, is linear and serial—dealing with one train of thought at a time; and it is limited in how much can be held in mind, a limitation of your working memory[2].

Conscious processing

This is not to deny that your conscious processing has its uses. For example, when learning a new motor skill, such as how to play a piano. At first you have intense conscious involvement in making each choice of what keys to press, when and with which fingers, to obtain each combination of notes. Agonizingly slow and deliberate whether starting with 'Chopsticks' or moving on to 'Für Elise'. But after a while, with repeated practice, what happens? You run through the melodies without a second thought. It's almost as if someone else is calling the tune. Yep. And that someone is *me*. Once movement sequences become automatic, you know who's running them. I devote nearly 70 billion neurons to such activity.

But conscious involvement in making decisions is also useful where there is a need for what are called propositional rules. These are the sort of rules we apply when we are doing arithmetic. I can do simple arithmetic such as nine times eight because I have internalized my multiplication tables from a great deal of recital during my early education. But anything more complicated such as 91 divided by 83—no way. You need to consciously *apply the rules* for long division!

Nevertheless, my job is to gather information about the world and steer your behavior appropriately. The neuroscientist David Eagleman in *The Brain, the Story of You* points out that it doesn't matter if your conscious awareness is involved or not and most of the time it's not. As he says, most of the time you are not aware of the decisions being made on your behalf. I do the work and then present solutions to your consciousness. Some writers describe this as like the brain having a competing group of solutions and the 'loudest shouter' amongst them wins the solution contest. The solutions do not emerge from a conscious process but are eventually *associated with* such a process. Thus in resolving the tempting choice of eating chocolate or doing without, "Eat the chocolate!" may be a louder shouter than "Do without!" It is perhaps rather ironic that we sometimes refer to an obvious choice as a 'no-brainer'—when it is the insistent result of my activity that has produced that very choice! Pah! No-brainer indeed.

Moral choice and accountability

Now it might sometimes happen that what I have assimilated through all the information that I have taken in over time leads me to a decision which is at odds with what you consider to be your moral principles. I may have processed subtle cues at an unconscious level and then delivered an 'informed' choice into your consciousness without your being able to justify that choice. Left to my own devices I might trigger behaviour that you would otherwise regret. For example, I might conclude that falsifying my tax return would be distinctly to my advantage. But your moral principles might be against such a decision. A conflict will result.

The assumption that you make conscious choices and that you are *responsible* for the decisions you make, lies at the heart of our notions of morality, of our legal system and of how we relate to one another. But is choice really 'free', or are you in some sense a slave to the 'decisions' that I make? So should I (your brain) take the blame rather than you?

Well your choice may not so much be 'free' from my 'decisions'—but rather it must be recognized that my decisions are *modifiable*. Your personal sense of the value of alternative actions emerges from life experience—interactions with the physical and social worlds 'out there'. Out of these interactions you normally arrive at some set of values, a moral code that differentiates between the good and the bad. In early moral development this differentiation is largely based on what behaviour has been rewarded and what has been punished. But when you get to around 11 years of age what is good and bad is represented by more abstract principles, such as those advocated in the world's religions. In addition, you may empathize with the *unpleasant* experiences of others, particularly if you have caused them, and recognize that this is 'not a good thing'. With such reflection you may arrive at a principle such as 'do unto others as you would be done by', for example.

Now all of this is reducible to representations in me, your brain. Your behaviour and conscious experience derive from what is activated at any given moment. Since those representations result from direct and second-hand experience, the moral choices you make will be a function of those experiences. Thus moral choice is modifiable—depending on what has been directly experienced and what has been learned. Other people largely determine that experience as well as education from the earliest years. This becomes supplemented by the institutions of formal education and, for many people, the institutions of their religious culture(s). Emotions such as empathy and sympathy will further shape moral choices.

So it could be argued that a failure in the moral choices I

make is in a sense a reflection of a failed society—one that has failed to provide the necessary life experiences for me to construct a moral conscience. I wire myself to the social reality I experience. "Hey, I got a social disease!" sings Riff, the *West Side Story* character in the song 'Gee, Officer Krupke', as an explanation for his 'delinquency'. Somewhat with tongue in cheek, he blames his delinquency on a failed society rather than his personal moral weakness.

But if you, the self-construct, are simply associated with the unconscious choices I have made 'autonomously', is it then appropriate to punish misdemeanours by punishing the person as represented by you, the self? Would it not make more sense to deal with deviant behaviour by further educating me, your brain? The concept and practice of rehabilitation are clearly consistent with this implication.

Avoiding cognitive dissonance

But you might justifiably ask if the concept of personal responsibility has evaporated with this analysis. That 'inner voice' of conscience is most definitely linked to the construct of you. Although it has no face, you hear it as *your* voice. So through that connection the conscious 'self' can in a sense be held to account, but rather more like a witness than an accomplice (and even then of course your 'self' is no more than yet another construction in me, the brain). So the question may be phrased as whether it is possible for the values and principles intimately connected to the construct of 'you' to somehow modify *my* activity—and this boils down to one set of brain processes influencing another set.

Think of it this way. What happens if I 'autonomously' attempt to initiate a behaviour which is at odds with those values and principles to which the construct of you is attached so intimately? I will create a state of dissonance, a conflict between my choice and 'your' principles. And this in turn will undermine the integrity of the construct of you, the self. But you know what, I am disposed to avoid such dissonance. I will try to find ways around it. You see I cannot deal with internal representations which are in conflict, which are not consistent with each other, like my impulse to act one way and the representation of you intimately linked to a morally preferable alternative. It's just the way I am. You can see why that makes sense. Imagine having to keep in mind millions of propositions which are inconsistent with each other. Such as 'the earth is a sphere *and* is flat'. Or 'the earth is the centre of the universe *and* a satellite of one star in the Milky Way galaxy'. Or 'the earth is cooling *and* the earth is warming'. And so on. And on. It simply couldn't work, could it. And it is this disposition to avoid such dissonant representations that provides the route through which the self-construct of you can *influence* me, your brain. Associating the self with a set of values and moral principles has the effect of constraining what I might otherwise do in pursuit of my evolutionary mission.

We can see a reference to this process in many phrases used to judge a person's behaviour from a moral perspective: 'letting *yourself* down', 'forgetting *yourself*', 'not being true to *yourself*'. Indeed the very concept of personal integrity alludes to the consistency with which a person adheres to their moral principles and values. So the construct of self, with its strong connectedness to a representation of values, can influence my decisions because I abhor dissonance and do not, as it were, want to undermine my construct of you, of the self. From this perspective, then, what the self represents can be held to account. We can perhaps hang on to the concept of personal responsibility after all. Phew! A rather lengthy argument to put across, but personal responsibility for one's actions is rather important for society to work.

The continuous activation of the internal representation of you, the self, generates the illusion of *you* being in control of elements of consciousness. That 'you' must over time become closely linked to a vast proportion of my representation of the world 'out there', and importantly to my emotional experience. Internal representations 'drive' my decision making, solving the problem of choice, but all the while giving the impression that that choice is made by the conscious self, by you. Sorry to have to confess to deluding you in that way. But let's not forget one thing. We need to revise the idea that conscious deliberation is the 'holy grail' of decision making. As you can see from this confession, occasionally conscious thought is helpful, but most of the time unconscious thought prevails. I decide for you—but allow you to take all the credit (and all the blame).

5

CONFESSION FIVE: AHEAD OF THE GAME

Prediction mode

Surprise! Who hasn't had innumerable surprises in their lives—from accidentally knocking over a glass of beer, to running across an old friend, to one of those 'surprise parties', of which some people live in utter dread. Well have you ever worked out what makes for a surprise? Something happens which you didn't expect. But hang on. You don't go about your daily activities consciously expecting. But let me confess. I do. Yep, most of the time I am running a kind of fast-forward video of what is going to happen next. I kind of live in a future which I anticipate is just about to happen. I continuously forecast what the immediate world will be like about 200 msec ahead of actuality[1]. I can do this, of course, because I am using my internal representation of the world 'out there'. That is what informs my expectations.

Now, why should I bother to operate this way, rather than live in the present. Well, as you know by now, my task is to guide the body I control through this world so that eventually

I survive to reproduce myself successfully. One way of dealing with this task is to try to stay one step ahead of potential disaster. Anticipation enables me to react more quickly and usually more appropriately. So bring it on—I am ready for it!

In fact, because I need some time to get information in and deal appropriately with it, I have delegated some escape responses to the spinal cord itself. If you put your hand on something hot you will have withdrawn it from the burning object before I know what has happened. It's called a spinal reflex and it operates without my involvement. Cut me off altogether and it will still happen on its own. You can appreciate its advantages.

Now back to my prediction mode. When my expectations are not confirmed, when the unexpected happens, three consequences are triggered. The first is that the 'surprise' leaps into consciousness and displaces whatever you were consciously processing at the time. I prioritize the happening in your ongoing conscious experience. The second is that a rather sophisticated series of bodily responses occur to help me deal with the surprise. Things like an increase in my sensory sensitivity, a brief constriction of my peripheral blood vessels and a redistribution of blood to the muscles and internal organs. Things like an increase in the tension of skeletal muscles and a brief increase in sweat-gland activity. If the surprise is strong enough to be called a startle, then there is also a release of adrenalin, which increases alertness, boosts energy in case I have to get into fight or flight mode and helps blood clotting should I get injured. All these adaptive changes are collectively called the orienting response, described as the 'what is it?' reflex, by the Russian physiologist Ivan Pavlov (1849–1936), an early investigator of the phenomenon.

Apart from monopolizing consciousness and triggering

the orienting response the unexpected can also modify future expectations. It does this by updating my internal representation of the world out there. Not surprisingly (!) this is especially likely to happen if the surprise event becomes the new normal. So in general what usually happens is that my expectations or predictions are more-or-less correct, and are thus continuously reinforced. But when particular surprises occur regularly, they update my internal representation and become the new prediction.

It should be noted that a violation of expectation, a surprise, is of course not necessarily related to a threat, it can be a delight. And much humour relies on such a violation of expectations—so long as the surprise is not at all threatening. This can be something like a circus clown appearing to throw a bucket of water over some spectators—but the content turns out to be confetti. We see it also in the use of puns, words with more than one meaning. Take for example this quip from Groucho Marx: "Outside of a dog, a book is man's best friend. Inside of a dog it's too dark to read". Just to bore you with the obvious (OK, I'm drilling down to what's happening here), 'outside' initially carries the meaning of 'other than', setting up one expectation—but then continues with its alternative meaning of 'a relative position in space'. Here's another pun: "Will glass coffins be a success? Remains to be seen". Yes, the amusement can sometimes be expressed in groans ...

Virtual reality

Now related to dealing as quickly as possible with whatever the world throws at me (confetti or not), I have to make another confession. You see, if every time my sense organs are stimulated by whatever is out there I had to synthesize all the information and put it together as something I recognized as a threat or opportunity—it would take a week and a day. That venomous snake would have given me a lethal bite before I had any idea what was going on. So I do not rely in each waking moment on a complete synthesis of incoming sensory information to reconstruct the world 'out there'. Rather I use fragmentary bits of sensory information. These serve to activate a more complete representation in my internal 'model' of the world. I don't bother to process all that sensory input. I will typically take in just enough to confirm my prediction and fill the gaps, as it were, by activating particular parts of my internal representation.

A good example of this process is the sensory experience of seeing. As described by Daniel Dennett, the American philosopher and cognitive scientist in *Consciousness Explained*:

> ... all vision except two or three degrees around dead center is normally concealed from us by the fact that our eyes, unlike television cameras, are not steadily trained on the world but dart in an incessant and largely unnoticed game of visual tag with the items of potential interest happening in our field of view.

As your brain I do the rest by activating the relevant parts of my internal representation, making the best guess about what I am seeing. It's the same with hearing and the other sensory modalities. It is this activation that generates your overall conscious experience: the perception of what you are sensing. As described in *Life of Brain*, it is estimated that only between 10 and 20 per cent of the information I use in 'seeing' actually comes from the eyes themselves. The rest comes from other parts of me, your brain. I predict far more visual input than I receive. Thus perhaps it is not surprising that about a third of the 'cerebral' part of me, the cortex[2], yes almost a *third*, is dedicated to the mission of vision.

Modern technology exploits this process by orchestrating sensory input to generate the experience of a virtual reality. Immersed in such a reality you are presented with a flow of stimuli, which give just enough information to trigger particular elements of your internal representations. However, as you can now appreciate after hearing my confession—*it is reality itself that is virtual*.

The virtual world of language

Now I have to bring to your attention yet another virtual reality, and that is the virtual world provided by language.

External stimuli arising from the world 'out there' directly activate my internal representations. A cat meanders into my field of vision and the stimulation of the visual system virtually instantaneously activates the internal representation of 'cat'. This is how I see a cat is 'out there', even though this is *all* just happening in me, your brain.

But let's say the cat is off chasing mice, no longer directly stimulating your visual system. Now if you read (or hear) the word 'cat', this word can activate some of those same internal representations that the cat 'out there' previously activated. In this way language can 'stand in' for the object (or event or action) represented by its word. So 'traffic jam' stands in for that frequent pastime of relaxing in your car and sharing the experience with hordes of other motorists. Great! With language you don't have to be there to enjoy the experience. This is how language frees me from having to have actual things right there in front of me in order to experience them.

Now language-driven experience is not quite the same thing as the original experience. Not quite so intense or detailed. More like shades of grey than vibrant colour. 'Traffic jam' doesn't yield the same ecstatic pleasure as the real thing. But it does provide a handy version. The main point is that conscious experience of the world through language does not need activation by the things 'out there' which originally created the experience. In this way language provides a *separate layer* of conscious representation.

Think of a sentence. When you read (or hear) it, it acts rather like a computer software program. Each word activates its internal representation and those representations are combined and interact in a particular way, depending on the grammatical structure of the sentence. *Jack and Jill went to the supermarket*. The words create a new internal representation, albeit usually only temporarily. This confers on language a virtually unrestricted freedom for thought, imagination and problem solving: a virtual world with limitless opportunities for reorganizing how the concepts of our internal representation can be arranged, can be related to each other. The linguistic level of consciousness is the foremost liberating force of freedom from direct experience. It provides a kind of theatre of the mind.

A phenomenal advantage of the use of language to capture the elements of our internal representations is that we can share those representations with others. This process can be particularly useful for the child learning new concepts because words invite infants to search for similarities amongst objects that might initially appear to their brains to be wildly dissimilar (e.g. toothbrush, clothes brush, sweeping brush, nail brush).

By verbally communicating elements of our own representations to others who know the same language, we can expand and modify their internal representations. This process frees us all from the limitations of our direct, personal experience. Thus our internal representation of the world 'out there' becomes not only a function of that experience, but also of the internal representations of others. This is how we share knowledge. This is how successive generations can build on the experience of their predecessors. This is how we have been so successful that we can now take 'time out' from the challenges of pure survival. As your brain I can now occupy myself with the other, symbolic world of thought, imagination, planning, creation. Your consciousness can then turn from the challenges of its evolution-defined mission to exploration of the *possible*. The words of the poet, novelist, playwright, indeed any storyteller, take you to new and fictional worlds, all the time activating elements of your internal representation and rearranging them in particular ways. A world of fiction abstracted from your world of 'reality'. And because words provide such versatile elements for internal manipulation, for holding many elements up in the air at once, so to speak, language provides a versatile medium for solving problems 'in the head'.

Your consciousness of a symbolic world based on language is experienced as an 'inner voice', that voice-without-a-face. This voice can describe thoughts, imagined things, future plans and the results of many other cognitive processes. Like my representation of the world 'out there', this consciousness is still represented internally as activated neural circuits—but mainly by representations of the symbols of language[3].

This inner voice should not be conceived as a separate entity, like a homunculus (dwarf) sitting in your brain and speaking to you. Rather it represents my activity and I am specifically employing language units to represent that activity to your consciousness.

This process is intimately linked to my representation of you, the construct of self. And to such an extent that you experience your *self* as hearing the inner voice, your *self* as thinking in words and sentences and so on. Effectively my cognitive operations, using the symbols of language and the construct of the self, seem to be merged into an integrated entity. The results of what I am engaged in and the activation of the self becoming part of the same event. The conscious you is then integrated with the conscious output of my activity. In the same way, my representation of plans and goals, ambitions, preferences, wishes, values, inhibitions and so on become wedded to my construct of you—the self. To a certain extent, you and I may then be regarded as acting as one.

Now language, this virtual level of representation, has many uses over and above the sharing of what is in one person's brain with that of another. It has enabled individuals to *coordinate* their activities. In this way the chances of survival of the lone individual are immensely improved by being part of a cohesive group. And once operating as a group, language provides a medium for the social rules that regulate and stabilize social behaviour—underpinning that inner voice of conscience.

And one other thing. As I mentioned in an earlier confession, language greatly facilitates learning of new actions, new response sequences, and directing them. Just as an external voice can direct us, such as a command from a sergeant major or a set of instructions for how to use that veritable explosion of functions provided by your new smartphone or computer, so can our inner voice, leading us by the verbal hand of language.

So we can now think of me, your brain, as functioning in three different worlds. First there is the immediate world 'out there', represented by the energy stimulating my receptors. Second there is the virtual world of my internal representations (which 'interpret' that sensory stimulation). And third there is the abstract world represented by the symbols of language (mainly)—a further virtual world.

Pitfalls of language

Despite all its unquestionable benefits language can have its drawbacks. For a start another person can use language to deceive us with lies rather than truth. And with the rapid rise of interconnectedness through new technologies we have witnessed the growth of incidents of fake news. Unfortunately the mere repetition of a false statement, such that it feels the more familiar, increases its likelihood of being believed.

When limited education results in an *exclusive world view* as a dominant feature of a person's internal representation of the world 'out there', it will inevitably also be closely associated with that person's representation of the self—and indeed perhaps reside at its very core. Confrontation by other, radically different alternative world views must be felt as a major challenge to that sense of self, threatening to demolish it.

Take *exclusive* exposure to a particular religion, for example (we could just as easily use as an example a particular political system). Persecution of others in the name of religion is a recurrent theme in history (religious wars account for only about seven per cent of recorded historical conflicts). Even in this modern era, in the year 2015, Christians were persecuted in 128 countries, Muslims in 125 and Jews in 74[4]. All this lack of tolerance of different religious beliefs is perhaps more about the defence of the self by the persecutors than a defence of a set of religious doctrines and beliefs. And who has not felt the tension of involvement in a task or other 'target of judgment', where that judgment is significant for one's self-esteem. Who has not felt more than a little defensive!

Even without an exclusive world view, I am quite capable of constructing an internal representation of values which may be quite at odds with my evolution-tied disposition to protect myself and my body—my innate dispositions to avoid harm and to seek nourishment. Driven by such abstract representation of ideals and values and principles, we have seen many humans engage in self-deprivation, from putting up with excruciating pain under torture and self-induced starvation, to taking the ultimate options of suicide or martyrdom. Such extremes are obviously in conflict with my fundamental mission of survival. Thus although language enhances social cohesion and can contribute in so many ways to increased survival, it also has the potential to represent a different reality, one that is in conflict with evolutionary forces.

Irrespective of education, most of us end up with some level of cultural conditioning, a strong cultural influence on our internal representation of the world 'out there'. Take for example the capitalist, free-market economic system with a virtually universal commitment to the politics of economic growth. In such a culture it is typical for the main news bulletin every day to include information about the status of stock market indices at home and abroad. Changes in the value of invested funds are of importance not just to fund holders but also for their implications for economic growth and development.

Stepping out of this sense of what the world is all about is not easy. We really need to make an effort to consider alternatives. And of course there are, such as a zero-growth economy, or even one with negative growth. We might consider such 'radical' ideas as a way of responding to continuing pressure on ever-decreasing resources, to damage of the environment, to global climate change, to pandemics and to the growing stresses on the workforce of the competitive model of the free market.

There is also a potential effect of what goes out in the news on our internal representation of the world 'out there'. If editorial policy focuses on the negative: conflicts around the world, terrorist attacks, violent crime, failures of the officers and machinery of state and so on, we the listeners and viewers can inadvertently develop a rather pessimistic representation. This is serious enough for psychologists to identify it as a 'mean world' syndrome.

And one final thing. When it comes to your needs and your preferences you can do more than just go after them. You can also *describe* them. And in doing that what do you do? You associate them with words that represent the self: the 'I' and 'me' of self-reference. Normally you don't just say "like cheese and bacon on my burger; don't like ketchup" but "*I* like cheese and bacon on my burger; *I* don't like ketchup." Language gives you that voice-without-a-face to represent all those needs and values and imaginings and plans. And in so doing it reinforces the illusion that there is an 'I' in conscious control. I confess that this illusion is all my fault. One way of countering it is to remind yourself that your apparent control is the result of activity in not one but two sources—the autonomous functioning of me, your brain, and the simultaneous activation of my internal representation of you, the construct of the self.

So as not to lose sight of this, perhaps you should start using the 'royal we'. You can start practising right now if you like. Just say to yourself: "*We* (my brain and its construct of *moi*) have just finished hearing this confession".

6
___

CONFESSION SIX: QUESTIONS

Now I have to advise you, in case you're not already aware, that there are some really important questions about consciousness that I have not yet addressed. The reason is, I have to confess, that I simply don't know the answers. And as far as I know, no-one else does either.

Really important question number one

"What are these important questions?" I hear you ask. Well here's the first and fundamental one. My functioning, as your brain, is physical. I consist of billions of richly interconnected nerve cells[1], as you already know, which have an impressive range of functions. Functions such as transmitting information from sense organs, activating muscles and glands, representing information temporarily in working memory and more-or-less permanently in long-term memory. They also function to create concepts and relations between them, to generate and interpret language, to solve problems, to create an internal representation of the world 'out there'—and to anticipate what's coming next. All these things you know your brain can do.

But there's one other really important function and that is to generate consciousness, your conscious experience. But there's a bridge to be crossed here—from the physical, tangible action of nerve cells to the 'spiritual', intangible experience of consciousness; from something that is most definitely material to something which most definitely is not.

There are a number of attempts currently in progress to cross this bridge. I shall very briefly mention three which seem to be receiving more than a little attention and which start from very different perspectives.

The first relates to the realm of quantum mechanics— that domain of physics which deals with the very small. You may need to take a deep breath before you take on board the next bit. Contemporary quantum mechanics argues that nothing 'exists' until one lot of energy interacts with another. It's a bit like an object (in quantum physics regarded as a bundle of energy) in a dark room only coming into existence when a beam of light energy bounces back off it into your eyes (eventually yielding you seeing the object). With this perspective, reality is no more than a variable flux (flow) of interacting energy, a kind of network of *relations* that weaves the world.

Now what we do is slice up that 'reality' into objects. For example, a chair (or any other apparent object) is not really an object in and of itself. Rather it is a localized field of energy that interacts with our sensory systems. We slice off this field of energy and consolidate it as a separate entity in our internal representations—in order to adapt to it. Although a chair may simply be conceived as energy vibrating somewhere in a much wider field of energy, that conception is not a lot of use. But slicing that energy up in such a way that we construe the energy as an object to sit on and take the weight off our feet—well that is!

Interestingly this could almost be a perfect description of the extensive and gradual process of learning about the world 'out there' as I, your brain, interact with it during development from neonate to adulthood. I am disposed to identify constancies and patterns and slice up the world in such a way that I can respond to it adaptively, consistent with my evolutionary mission.

Simply stating 'quantum effects cause consciousness' obviously explains nothing until someone can specify how. And the idea that consciousness *requires* quantum processes has made virtually no progress to date because there is so little evidence of relevant quantum processes in the brain. And this is because physics, at whatever level of enquiry, is concerned with matter, yet the fundamental properties of consciousness are not material but spiritual (in the sense of that intangible 'essence of experience'). As the British philosopher Philip Goff in *Galileo's Error: Foundations for a New Science of Consciousness* puts it:

> ... the purely quantitative science of Galileo cannot capture the qualitative reality of subjective consciousness ... Physical science restricts itself to providing information about the behaviour of the things it talks about—particles, fields, space-time—and tells us nothing about their intrinsic natures[2] ... there must be more to what an electron is than what it does.

Nevertheless, as expressed in *Life of Brain*, there is something rather appealing about the idea that the variable flux of the outer world is represented by the variable flux of the inner world—the complex network of interactions arising from the interconnectedness of the billions of neurons which constitute our internal representation, our personal reality. Somehow this flux engenders the various aspects of consciousness. But quantum mechanics cannot tell us how.

The second idea for crossing that bridge between the material and spiritual has been advanced in particular by Guilio Tononi and Christof Koch. They call it 'Integrated Information Theory'. Their notion is that any system at all could be conscious—providing that the information it contained is sufficiently interconnected and organized—as in the human brain. To quote from one of their scientific papers "... any physical system with some capacity for integrated information would have some degree of experience, irrespective of the stuff of which it is made ..." As described in *Life of Brain*, in this context, 'information' means how much the system in question constrains its own past and future possibilities. 'Integrated' means how much the information in the system is dependent on interconnection between parts of the system. And we need to add one further condition—'maximality'. A system is conscious when it has a *maximum* of integrated information (i.e. not surpassed from below or above). As Philip Goff puts it, "A brain is plausibly a maximum of integrated information, as it neither contains nor is contained within something with a greater level of integrated information."

That means not just your brain, but perhaps your laptop, mobile phone, a robot, the Internet, a city, or even the planet *could* have some degree, some form of consciousness. And given that at a subatomic level a stone may be described as having integrated information, that too may have some form of consciousness!

It is rather too early (and perhaps too challenging) to evaluate evidence for their proposition, but let us just suggest in passing that Koch and Tononi are really arguing from analogy, a potentially precarious path for the creative imagination to take. Their theory emerges from an examination of some abstracted properties of the conscious brain and from which they infer that other systems with such properties must also have some kind or degree of consciousness. In attributing consciousness to interconnected information systems with the properties they propose, they have created their own construct of consciousness. There is nothing wrong with this of course, but to paraphrase a famous line from the 1987 song by The Firm (which parodies the first science fiction series *Star Trek*)—"It's consciousness, Jim, but not as we know it".

The third bridge is perhaps the most radical of all and is known as panpsychism, a theory eloquently elaborated by Philip Goff, amongst others. He starts with the idea that consciousness—and by this he means experience—is unobservable. It is only known to the conscious, experiencing being. You can observe someone smelling a rose, but you cannot observe their experience of the scent. Next it is proposed that there is a continuum of consciousness, with humans at an advanced level, but gradually decreasing in richness and complexity in progressively simpler forms of life.

At this point in the argument there is perhaps the most radical assertion: this continuum carries on from organic to inorganic matter. Yep—from living creatures to inanimate objects such as a stone. Echoes of Koch and Tononi at this point! And the continuum doesn't stop there. It goes on right down to fundamental particles such as quarks and electrons. They will be characterized by incredibly simple forms of experience, which are frankly rather hard to imagine, but there you are.

Philip Goff observes in his quotation earlier that physical science is confined to telling us about what matter does. But it tells us nothing about the intrinsic nature of matter—what it is in and of itself. Panpsychism asserts that this intrinsic nature *is* consciousness. Thus consciousness is a quality inherent to all matter—a fundamental feature that permeates the universe.

At one level this theory is very seductive. The question of how consciousness emerges from neural activity ceases to be a problem. All matter has consciousness but to different degrees of complexity and richness. End of. Job done.

But the problem is how on earth can this theory be tested? Because consciousness cannot be observed in another person, let alone in a rock or an electron, we have no way of evaluating its validity. Thus panpsychism becomes a matter not of fact, but more of a philosophical stance in relation to a metaphysical problem—one might almost say, a matter of belief.

For what it's worth I have to propose a rather less radical belief. Specifically that consciousness is an *intrinsic property* of certain patterns of activity in me, your brain. That statement represents the very limit of my capability of understanding.

Now this may sound like a complete cop-out. But let's just look briefly at quantum mechanics once more and we'll see at its very foundation there is also an acceptance of *intrinsic* properties. Take the proton, for example, one of the three particles that make up atoms. Protons have a property called 'spin' and the direction and strength of this property determine the proton's magnetic and electrical properties. This 'spin' is the result of the activity of even smaller fundamental particles that make up the proton called quarks and gluons. Quarks (a nonsense word which appears in James Joyce's

Finnegan's Wake) appear to contribute about 30 per cent of proton 'spin' and gluons (from glue + on) about 40 per cent. But the point is that this property of 'spin' is the *intrinsic* angular momentum inherent to any fundamental particle[3]. So a fundamental property of what ultimately makes up the universe is regarded as an intrinsic property, requiring no further 'explanation'.

So perhaps it is not a meaningful question to ask *how* consciousness arises from neuronal activity. Let's call it an intrinsic property. Let's just accept it as a *Dark Process*.

Really important question number two

The second important question about consciousness, about which I have thus far remained rather quiet, is this. Why does experience take the *form* it does? Why should something 'hot' feel hot? After all, at a microscopic level the conduction of heat from a hot body to you is actually the transfer of *kinetic* energy from rapidly moving atoms and molecules. Heat is the energy of movement! It is my interpretation or rather transformation of that energy that creates the sensation of heat. In the same way, why are colours experienced the way they are when they are really variations in the wavelength of light energy? Why do the vibrations of air molecules arriving at the ear sound like, well, sound? And so on with all of our sensations. They are transformations that do not reside in the nature of the original stimulus. Had humans evolved with different brains, vibrations of air molecules might just as easily have been experienced as different colours[4]; and different colours experienced as, well, different sounds.

I have suggested earlier that the *function* of my transformations may be to aid in both the discrimination and internal representation of the different stimuli arriving at the different sense receptors. But that is rather speculative. And anyway, it doesn't go anywhere near explaining the different *qualities* of sensory experience, of explaining the origins of my particular transformations. Sorry, can't help you there.

Really important question number three

The third question we have not yet addressed is this. Why is it that some of my activity is conscious—what you experience —while other of my activity, in fact most of it, is not? Well one thing is that if you were conscious of everything I do your consciousness would be absolutely overwhelmed. If you think of the contents of consciousness at any one time a bit like following a particular route on a road to somewhere, then the contents of what I do would be like simultaneously trying to follow thousands of routes all at the same time. You see the problem.

Now I have mentioned to you earlier that the basic properties of conscious experience are related to my survive-to-reproduce mission. Whence consciousness of sensory input in real time; consciousness of rapid interpretation of that input by reference to my internal representation of the world 'out there'; consciousness of the emotional meaning of that interpretation (is it painful, is it pleasure through reduction of need?); and consciousness of motivational implications (escape or avoidance of pain, approach to opportunities to satisfy needs?).

I have also mentioned to you earlier that my construct of the self, of you, seems to be intimately tied to all of these things. The self experiences the real-time sensations, the perceptions of what's out there, the emotions associated with these perceptions. I have been a little disparaging about this. As if I am a little peeved at the self 'taking over' my activities.

But here's a suggestion. My construct of the self is an 'integrating construct', as concluded in confession two, a construct that links my identity with a body and my interactions with that body, whether exclusively internal—or in directing its engagement with the world 'out there'. But perhaps the self is even more integrative than I thought. Perhaps the self *is* the conscious element of my survival activity. After all, in fulfilling my evolutionary destiny I must look after not just myself, your brain, but also the body. I must look after what is represented by the integrated self-construct.

What I am trying to suggest is that the integrated self comes into its own as the focus of conscious experience in adapting to the world 'out there'. So not just consciousness but consciousness of self become part of the frontline of my survival battle.

And one last point in relation to this notion. Perhaps the conscious self also comes into its own not just as me trying to optimize chances of survival but also in relation to others. After all, I have to differentiate between me—body and mind if you like—and others, just as they have to differentiate me from themselves. So this social context defining me (and you!) reinforces the identity of the self I have created. And we all know how important others can be in shaping, developing and sometimes undermining our sense of who we are.

So you almost become the conscious processes which represent my survival priorities. You represent the whole of which I have to defend and nourish. You are what enables a clear distinction between me and others. And once the self has been constructed, the story of consciousness becomes the story of the self. No wonder you think it's all about you! Now you are not by any measure the whole of me—but from a survival perspective, you have a rather important role. In this role the self, I am suggesting, becomes the conscious me.

So here's a revised and now more complimentary version of my earlier paraphrase (at the end of confession two) of those famous lines by William Shakespeare in *Macbeth*:

> *Self's but a mental construct, like* all *else,*
> *But serves survival, taking up the guise*
> *Of consciousness in readiness for threat*
> *Or opportunity for meeting needs—*
> *The guardian of the brain.*

AFTERWORD

Well, there you are. That's me owned up to all those deceptions, illusions and confusions. I've developed human consciousness and the construct of you, the self. Together, me your brain and my construct of you, we have overcome the challenges of survival. In my current version for over 300,000 years. Not bad, eh? Mind you, that's nothing compared with our ancestors *Homo erectus*. They successfully continued on this planet for almost two *million* years! Will we do as well as them and keep going past the year 1,500,000?

Hmmm.

ACKNOWLEDGMENTS

Thanks to Sara Fuller and my wife, Amanda Windsor, who urged me to write for a wider audience. I am also indebted to readers of this book who gave invaluable feedback during its development, in particular Stephen Agar, Andy Woods and several members of my family: Rupert, Barbara, Marcus and Tom Fuller. I gratefully acknowledge also the expert professional help given by my editor Jane Woodhead.

Any errors are of course my responsibility.

REFERENCES

Bryson, B. (2019). *The Body. A Guide for Occupants*. Doubleday, London.

Coppens, Y. cited in Hanks, J. (2019). *Finding Lucy*. In French Living—Connexion, September 2019, 8–9.

Delmonte, M.M. and Halpin, M. (2019). *Evolution and Consciousness*. Koninklijke Brill, Leiden.

Dennett, D.C. (1993). *Consciousness Explained*. Penguin Books, London.

de Waal, F.B.M. (2019). *Mama's Last Hug: Animal Emotions and What They Tell Us About Ourselves*. W.W. Norton & Company, New York.

Eagleman, D. (2015). *The Brain: The Story of You*. Canongate Books, Edinburgh.

Fuller, R. (forthcoming). *Life of Brain*. Austin Macauley Publishers, London.

Gladwell, M. (2006). Blink. *The Power of Thinking Without Thinking*. Penguin Books, London.

Goff, P. (2019). *Galileo's Error. Foundations For a New Science of Consciousness*. Pantheon Books, New York.

Gould, J.L. and Gould, C.G. (1994). *The Animal Mind*. Holt, New York.

James, W. (1890). *The Principles of Psychology* (rev. 1918). Pantianos Classics, Amazon Distribution, Leipzig.

Lemasson, A. (2019). *Connexion*, Nov. 2019, English Language Media Sarl, Monaco. p. 23.

Tononi, G. and Koch, C. (2008). *The Neural Correlates of Consciousness: An Update*. Annals of the New York Academy of Sciences. 1124: 239–261.

NOTES

2. Confession two: The Self

1. Thanks to Michael Delmonte and Maeve Halpin in *Evolution and Consciousness* for drawing my attention to this great quote of Freud's.

3. Confession three: Evolution of consciousness

1. The term hominin refers to members of the human side of this evolutionary split for whom we have fossil evidence.
2. Although brain size is not always a straightforward indicator of level of function.

4. Confession four: Who's in charge?

1. The dilation was induced by application of the drug atropine.
2. Working memory is a short-term memory where information is consciously represented for a brief time. It is consciously experienced as the psychological 'present'.

5. Confession five: Ahead of the game

1. As it happens, that may more-or-less coincide with the delay caused by the time needed to integrate information taking different amounts of time to arrive from the different senses.
2. Cortex literally meaning 'outer layer', as in bark on a tree.
3. Note that the world of symbols could also be mathematical or involve imagery or musical notation.
4. According to statistics from the Pew Research Centre, a non-partisan American 'fact tank'.

6. Confession six: Questions

1. We might note in passing that the human brain also has around the same number of glia (literally 'glue') cells as neurons. Originally thought to serve only to support the architecture of the neuronal system, it is now known that different types of glial cell also function as the brain's immune system, to maintain the working environment of nerve cells and even to modulate how nerve cells communicate.

2. In the sense of the irreducible essence of something that determines its properties.

3. Intrinsic Angular Momentum. Sciencedirect.com (2020), Elsevier B.V.

4. Interestingly about four per cent of people can experience synesthesia (experience of one sense triggered by stimulation of a different sense), the most common of this being chromesthesia: particular sounds involuntarily evoke the experience of particular colours. This colour experience does not displace the sound experience and may be seen 'in the mind's eye' or projected onto an external surface.

ABOUT THE AUTHOR

Ray Fuller taught Psychology for forty years at Trinity College Dublin. He retired to SW France to craft furniture and to write.

Website: rayfuller.ampbk.com

INDEX

Printed in Great Britain
by Amazon